# dear me

by Desiree Kose

*This book is dedicated to the young Polynesian girl that doesn't know her power yet.*

Dear Reader,

This is a collection of words that came to me in love, disobedience, unlearning, growing and faithfulness.

Read it straight through or shuffle. I hope it brings comfort and grows with you.

Your pace.

Love,
de.kose

# table of contents

**Book Dedication**
**Dear Reader Letter**
**Order of Words:**

**Your Best**

Your best is going to look different every day,
but as long as you do your best that's all anyone can ask of you.

**Growing Pains**

Self love and respecting your own boundaries will come with push back.
There's going to be a lot of times when you're going to have to take the high road.

Thats when you remember, "your peace, no one else's"

**Dating 101**

Have an exit strategy.

**You v You**

The world is gonna try to make you turn on your neighbor.
There is enough room out here for everyone.
It's always and only going to be - you v you.

Don't let the evil in others distract you from a blessed life.

**Yours to Take**

You don't have hide yourself to make others feel comfortable.
You worked hard to build yourself up to take up space – take it.

**Future Me**

The person you want to be also needs you.

**Pay No Mind**

Focus on your own pockets.
The outside noise is going to pressure your dollar.

Remember money will always look its best growing in your own accounts.

**Real Life**

Be weary of the likes.
The way you get them can easily be a weapon they use against you in the future.

**She is Healthy**

Being built like this is not unhealthy.
Health looks different for everyone.
Your body is built to last.

## Acceptance and Appreciation

I know we're all breaking childhood traumas especially around appearance.
Self love is probably the toughest love to come face to face with.

It's a daily thing. Let the process be a blessing.

**Why so Serious?**

Learn to not take yourself too serious but in the same breath take life serious.
Lean to the side of what brings joy over outside expectation.

**Don't take it Personal**

Allow people do what's best for them.
You don't have to be what's best for everyone.
Let that pressure go.

**Sticks & Stones**

Your feelings around the words that people say are valid but temporary.

**Take that Moment**

Whether you need 5 minutes, 10 minutes or an hour.
There's plenty of time in the day to get shit done.
Take your moment.

**After Love**

The only person that matters is you:
how you feel
how you heal
how you react
how you tolerate
how you leave
how you stay

You.

**After Love Pt. 2**

how you unlearn
how you relearn

**Lottery**

A whole walking lottery - you better act like you know.

**Code Switch**

The habits you've built having to live in survival mode
are a trap to keep you in that cycle.

Allow yourself to flow.

**How You**

Love how you love.

**Empty**

A reminder to free up space where they use to live:
mind
heart
journal
phone

take the trash out.

**Know Better**

it's one thing for them to underestimate you,
it's a whole other thing for you to underestimate yourself.

You know better.

**Warrented**

I don't "wish well" anymore.
It's overrated and 100% of the time not warranted.

**Gotta Be**

be bold
be confident
be vocal
be detailed

**Real Love**

There's no way around not loving yourself.

**Walk Away**

Give yourself permission to walk away first.

**Broke-n**

We don't talk enough about how much it sucks having to go to work with a broken heart.

**Fail Fast**

Try, fail – try again – fail again, reflect.

**Experience**

I don't wonder "why" anymore.

I know it's possible to fall too quickly,
I know it's possible to fall over time
and I know it's possible to fall by yourself.

**Hard Life**

Life is hard, yes, but it's also not as bad as the thoughts you believe it to be.

**KRM-a**

The silence was a ringing reminder of all the possibilities  that could of been and inevitably never was.

**A First**

Looking back, I didn't once imagine what a future with you would look like – a first.

That should of been my first caution sign.

**Know Now**

I was ready to choose a person and you showed up.
I know now that even things that come on time aren't always
going to last

**Single Match**

Something in me broke when you didn't want me anymore, there was nothing I could do and I wasn't going to fight for us alone.

**I Am**

As much as I know who I am, I still got lost in him.

**A Reminder**

Grace is for everyone – especially you.

**10/3/22**

Even when you know the truth, ask him for his truth.
Even when the hair isn't yours, ask him for his truth.
Even when you see the notif on his phone, ask for his truth.

Confirmation is powerful.
There's confidence in confirmation.

**Lean In**

There's no shame in having a very raw human experience.

## The Current

Flowing not floating.

**Grounding**

Some things deserve silence over solution

**Free Returns**

The hurt can only last as long as you allow it to sit with you. Send it back.

**Another Reminder**

Find the things that bring you unmatched joy.

**Gut Check**

What are you going back and forth for?
Why are you letting words sway you with no action?
Who is the prize?

**AM - PM**

Don't wait on any text to start and have a great day.
Don't wait on any text to end and have a good night.

**6/5/23**

2 things you learn about dating:
    1. people are going to project – don't take it personal.
    2. if you don't love yourself first – you will get used.

**1/30/22**

*I will always love you
I gave you real love and whether you know it or not
I was all about you.
Not once did I ever give up on you.
Not once did I ever want our relationship to end.*

*But I feel like you never really understood where I was coming from.*

**Show Love**

I don't ever want to feel like I have to hide love - protect love, of course.

But never hide it.

**The Ocean**

Love loudly and deeply.

**Unsent Text Pt.1**

I've written you so many letters to you in my head, some about love and some about goodbyes.

Regardless of the context, it was enough to understand that you were important to me and I think that's what's worth actually sharing.

**Self Love Letter Pt. 57**

You are so precious.
God is going to take care of you.

You're crying now but you'll be okay.
You'll forget about it and be open to love again.
Wholeheartedly.

Let go with ease, knowing that you tried to the end.

**Be Done**

Done with feeling like second best
Done with this attachment
Done with you

**Stand in Truth**

You being insecure is hindering your growth.
The gaslighting he projects is because he has something to hide.
Stand in your truth.

**Nxt**

You win, this time.
But I got next.

**In My Next**

My time will be respected
I will be prioritized
I will not have to beg
My love won't be taken for granted

**A Reminder Pt. 62**

You always figure it out.
Pray about it.
Stop the negative self talk.
Remember who you are.
Know your worth.

## A Tragedy

He was it.
He was my last love.

I was his.
I wasn't his only love.

**Haiku**

He didn't see me
He saw an accessory

He didn't love me
He loved his pride

**In n Out**

I can't remember the moment I fell in love,
but I'll never forget the time it took to fall out of love.

**Reminder 66**

Your doubt is distracting you from your destiny.

**Opportunities**

The opportunity to do something that nobody has ever done and to be great at it is available to everyone.

**A Day**

Have nothing left at the end of the day.
Earn your rest.

**Right Focus**

Focus on what you did do,
not what you didn't do.

**More Than One**

There are so many different ways to be successful.
Find what works for you.
Don't get caught up in distractions.
Enjoy the lane you're in.

**My Experience**

I would always get caught up with how people viewed me –
especially in the fashion industry.
I didn't grow up with a similar background to people who I went
to school with and I was usually the only Samoan in the rooms I
would walk into.
I had no legacy to follow, no money, no handouts
but I had heart – hella heart.

## Reflection

What it comes down to is what we're made of,
what the core of who we are looks like and
what we cling to when we get uncomfortable.

**Grounding Pt. 2**

Ground yourself, understand what keeps you together and hold on to that.

**Built Different**

You're built for your own legacy.
Working hard is great but working smart is better.
Have heart.

### Strength for the Storms

Don't pray for weaker storms,
pray for stronger faith to weather the storm.

## A Real Life Scenario

You found your stride, you're focused, locked in and then lift your head up and see people moving funny and it's gonna do 2 things;
1. Throw you off
2. Make you want to work harder.
I urge you to do 3 and rest in where you are at and take your time.

PLAY YOUR GAME.

**Make It**

I'm not in a rush to make it – I am confident in the work I'm doing and the work that I've done in the past to get me to where I am now.

**Owning It**

I take complete responsibility for myself, my actions and the words I speak/write.

The work that I need to do personally, financially, mentally, spiritually and for my community.

**Claim it**

I claim an abundance of love over myself and my actions so
fierce it scares me.

**Show Up**

Let love be enough.
It doesn't matter who doesn't show,
it matters if you show up for yourself.

**Unsolicited**

Just because you think you're what I need, doesn't mean that
you are. stop trying to convince me.

## He was It

He was it,
He was the one...
until he wasn't.

**Crying Over You**

I cry when I think about the imaginary life I planned for us.
I cry when I read our old text thread and remember how your
words would make me feel.
I cry when i imagine you talking to other women and that energy
i experienced being poured into someone who is not me.
I cry at the thought of you not thinking of me from time to time.

I cry over you.

## Hurting

I'm hurt that you stopped caring.
I'm hurt because I have to be strong.
I'm hurt because I let you hurt me.

**Final Goodbye EP**

Thankful For You - Skills ft. Des
Lost Puppy - Des ft. Rashad
Greatest Game Ever Played - Des ft. Reese
Free Ice Cream Dream - Des ft. Forrest
Lost In The Sauce - Des ft. Jo
Ghost in the Gym - Des ft. Karter

**Emotionless**

There's nothing left to feel.
Nothing to cling to
Not a word
Or an image to bring me back
No more.

**N.E**

You lied to me today, again…
But you tell my favorite lies

**Lyrics**

The only time you cross my mind is when you cross the line.

**Paths**

You can't explain your greatness to people, they need to
experience it for themselves.

**Let'em Talk**

I let you talk because you like talking,
not because I agree with everything you're saying

ʼ

**A Battle**

You don't go to war with people you have to question.

**Love Storage**

I want to be confident in where I store love.

**Stand Up**

Those experiences that build resilience are
going to feel the hardest to get through.

Don't let temporary pain define a fleeting moment.

**Renewed**

I've come to terms with the fact that,
I AM BUILT FOR THIS.

**New Love**

Look for a love that is inspired by you.
Look for a love that looks for you.

Dear Reader,

I'm holding back tears as I'm writing this last page.
I don't know who you are but I hope this book
found you during a time of growth and self discovery.
This collection of notes, journals, and prayers have been
hidden for a long time.

As I walk toward my calling,
I had to unhide my hurt.
In turn, I hope this inspires you to do the same.

Here's to walking in total truth.

Love,
de.kose

.

JOSHUA 10:25